A Time TO Heal

a grief journal

BETH MARSHALL

AMBASSADOR INTERNATIONAL
GREENVILLE, SOUTH CAROLINA & BELFAST, NORTHERN IRELAND

www.ambassador-international.com

A Time to Heal
a grief journal

Printed in the United States of America

ISBN: 978-1-935507-51-2

Cover Design & Page Layout by David Siglin of A&E Media

AMBASSADOR INTERNATIONAL
Emerald House
427 Wade Hampton Blvd.
Greenville, SC 29609, USA
www.ambassador-international.com

AMBASSADOR BOOKS
The Mount
2 Woodstock Link
Belfast, BT6 8DD, Northern Ireland, UK
www.ambassador-international.com

The colophon is a trademark of Ambassador

SPECIAL THANKS TO MY FRIENDS Jennifer Barden and Chris Dunagan for their editing and graphic design help, and endless encouragement. I will be forever grateful to my pastor and dear friend, Perry Noble for sharing the question, "what would you do for God if you knew you couldn't fail?" Perry, you've shown people all over the world to pray huge prayers, and trust Him for the rest.

And finally, I thank God for taking me from Atlanta to Boston to meet an amazing man from South Carolina, my husband! Paul, your love and support since Beazy's death and through the creation of A Time to Heal has been priceless. I love you more than you'll ever know.

On October 16, 2010, Paul's beloved mother, Mozelle Marshall passed away. Mozie's vibrant life and generous spirit will long live on through her children, grand and great grandchildren.

To God be the glory!

INTRODUCTION

The season following the death of a loved one is a time few of us are equipped to handle on our own. When you have loved deeply, it is very likely that your grief will also be deep.

You may have thought, "If I can just make it through the service, then I'll be okay." A few weeks go by, family gathers, friends visit, people call, and then reality begins to surface. For some it seems that the tears will never end. For others, you may be unable to cry. One thing is for certain, you are not alone. Our mighty God promises that He will never leave you.

My prayer is that by remembering, you will be comforted as your heart begins to heal.

THIS JOURNAL WAS WRITTEN AFTER the sudden death of a very special woman. Bea Montgomery Evans was a remarkable lady, mother, grandmother and friend. She was even a newlywed. The joy of her life and the kindness of her heart touched people in amazing ways. Since the time of her death, memories have been an important part of the healing process.

In Loving Memory of my mom,
Beazy

(Place a picture here

of the loved one

you are remembering

through this journal.)

MATTHEW 5:4
"Blessed are they who mourn;
for they shall be comforted."

THE STORY OF A LIFE is a treasure worth preserving. As you recall long ago and recent memories, you may want to write them here to help keep them fresh in your mind and close to your heart.

_____
_____
_____
_____
_____
_____
_____
_____
_____
_____
_____
_____
_____
_____
_____
_____
_____
_____
_____
_____
_____
_____
_____
_____
_____
_____

PHILIPPIANS 1:3

"I thank my God every time
I remember you."

FOR SOME, SHEDDING TEARS AND showing emotion come very naturally. For others, it may be difficult to admit that you're really not okay. Know that tears can cleanse like a refreshing rain. How are you coping today? Tell God what's on your heart, trusting that He is near.

PSALM 40:1

"I waited patiently for the Lord;
He turned to me and heard my cry."

THE DAY OF THE MEMORIAL service can be very painful. It can also be a special time to celebrate the life of someone you love. Reflecting is an important part of the healing process. Write the details you remember about the day of the service. Try to remember special music, people who were there and anything else that touched your heart.

_____

_____

_____

_____

_____

_____

_____

_____

_____

_____

_____

_____

_____

_____

_____

_____

_____

_____

_____

_____

_____

_____

_____

_____

_____

_____
_____
_____
_____
_____
_____
_____
_____
_____
_____
_____
_____
_____
_____
_____
_____
_____
_____
_____
_____
_____
_____
_____

2 CORINTHIANS 1:3-4

"Praise be to the God and Father of our Lord Jesus
Christ, the Father of compassion and the God of
all comfort, who comforts us in all our troubles, so
that we can comfort those in any trouble with the
comfort we ourselves have received from God."

WHETHER A PERSON DIES SUDDENLY or there's been time to prepare, you may have questions about death coming sooner or maybe even later than you expected. On these pages, take a moment and talk about the timing of your loved one's death. It's okay to be honest with God. Ask Him to pour out His blessings on you today, and to renew your strength.

_____
_____
_____
_____
_____
_____
_____
_____
_____
_____
_____
_____
_____
_____
_____
_____
_____
_____
_____
_____
_____
_____
_____
_____

ISAIAH 40:31

"Those who hope in the Lord will renew their strength.
They will soar on wings like eagles; they will run and
not grow weary, they will walk and not be faint."

WRITTEN MEMORIES ARE A GOOD way to keep someone close to your heart. What do you remember about the last time you were together with your loved one? Be sure to include where you were, who else was there and any conversations you can recall. Use these pages to preserve those memories.

PSALM 46:10

"Be still, and know that I am God..."

THERE ARE TIMES WHEN GRIEVING feels physically painful. During a season of grief, it may be hard to find the right words to pray. Tell God how you're feeling today. When words seem insufficient, know that God's Holy Spirit will intercede and pray for you in a way that is too awesome to understand. He knows your heart.

_____
_____
_____
_____
_____
_____
_____
_____
_____
_____
_____
_____
_____
_____
_____
_____
_____
_____
_____
_____
_____
_____
_____
_____
_____

ROMANS 8:26

"We do not know what we ought to pray for, but the
Spirit himself intercedes for us with groans that
words cannot express."

(Place a picture here

of the loved one

you are remembering

through this journal.)

MATTHEW 5:4
"Blessed are they who mourn;
for they shall be comforted."

T HERE MAY BE SOME THINGS you wish you had said to your loved one, or even some things you wish you had not said. Write down any regrets you have. If there is anything you want to forgive or be forgiven for, you may want to write about those things too. Ask God to heal those places in your heart and fill you with His peace.

DANIEL 9:9

"The Lord our God is merciful and forgiving..."

ALLOWING OTHERS TO SHARE YOUR sorrow can be a real source of support. How are you letting people know what's going on in your heart, that you're grieving the death of a loved one? Ask God to walk with you, knowing that healing is taking place in His perfect time.

WORRY, FEAR AND UNCERTAINTY ABOUT the future can seem overwhelming. You may feel that the mountains ahead of you are just too enormous. Know that they don't all have to be climbed today. Tell God about your fears and concerns with confidence that your prayers are being heard. Leave your troubles with Him as you rest in God's arms tonight.

_____
_____
_____
_____
_____
_____
_____
_____
_____
_____
_____
_____
_____
_____
_____
_____
_____
_____
_____
_____
_____
_____

PHILIPPIANS 4:6–7

"Do not be anxious about anything, but in everything,
by prayer and petition, with thanksgiving, present
your requests to God. And the peace of God, which
transcends all understanding, will guard your hearts
and minds in Christ Jesus."

DO YOU NEED SOME COMFORT today? Jesus healed people who were broken and alone. The same power that made a crippled man walk and a blind man see can heal your heart. He is able to break through the darkest clouds with His light. Ask Him to begin a mighty healing in your life. Be specific. Pray big. What do you want Him to do? As you write this prayer, remember that God's power is enormous—He created the entire universe.

_____
_____
_____
_____
_____
_____
_____
_____
_____
_____
_____
_____
_____
_____
_____
_____
_____
_____
_____
_____
_____
_____
_____
_____

MATTHEW 15:29-30

"Then He went up on a mountainside and sat down.
Great crowds came to Him, bringing the lame, the
blind, the crippled, the mute and many others and
laid them at his feet; and He healed them."

IT'S HARD TO FIND THE right words to say after a death. While trying to avoid causing additional pain, friends may be reluctant to talk about the person who has died. Ironically, sharing stories and reminiscing about happier times are some of the best ways to begin healing after a painful loss. What do you want people to know about your loved one? Use these pages to tell that story. Is there a person who seems to understand? If not, you can ask God to send someone. An empathetic friend is a true gift from God.

PHILIPPIANS 1:6

"...He who began a good work in you will carry it on
to completion until the day of Christ Jesus."

WHAT ARE SOME WAYS YOU can be good to yourself? Art, music and writing are excellent emotional outlets. You may enjoy walking, bike riding or other athletic activities. Spending time with encouraging people can lift your spirits. A warm bath can soothe a weary soul. Take a few minutes to write down some creative ways to pamper or take care of yourself.

"...I sing for joy at the works of your hands."

A S YOU TRAVEL THROUGH THE first year after the death of a loved one, you will undoubtedly learn a lot. You may discover strength and perseverance you didn't know you had. Occasionally you may feel a wave of grief that suddenly overwhelms you, and at other times, moments of pure unexpected happiness. Every person's journey is different. The next four pages are to record what you remember about the first twelve months. Be sure to notice the point when your heart starts to feel lighter and more joyful. Telling the story can help you heal.

PHILIPPIANS 4:13

"I can do everything through Him who gives me strength."

(Place a picture here

of the loved one

you are remembering

through this journal.)

MATTHEW 5:4
"Blessed are they who mourn;
for they shall be comforted."

_____
_____
_____
_____
_____
_____
_____
_____
_____
_____
_____
_____
_____
_____
_____
_____
_____
_____
_____
_____
_____
_____
_____
_____
_____
_____
_____
_____
_____

PHILIPPIANS 4:13

"I can do everything through Him who gives
me strength."

_____
_____
_____
_____
_____
_____
_____
_____
_____
_____
_____
_____
_____
_____
_____
_____
_____
_____
_____
_____
_____
_____
_____
_____

2 TIMOTHY 1:7

"For God did not give us a spirit of timidity, but a spirit of power, of love and of self-discipline."

MONTHS 7-9

_____
_____
_____
_____
_____
_____
_____
_____
_____
_____
_____
_____
_____
_____
_____
_____
_____
_____
_____
_____
_____
_____
_____
_____
_____
_____
_____
_____
_____
_____

PHILIPPIANS 4:19
"And my God will meet all your needs according to
His glorious riches in Christ Jesus."

_____
_____
_____
_____
_____
_____
_____
_____
_____
_____
_____
_____
_____
_____
_____
_____
_____
_____
_____
_____
_____
_____
_____
_____
_____
_____
_____

ROMANS 15:13

"May the God of hope fill you with all joy and
peace as you trust in Him, so that you may overflow
with hope by the power of the Holy Spirit."

THESE PAGES ARE FOR A special card, newspaper article, or other treasure you want to be sure and save. You may want to keep a box or envelope with this book for meaningful keepsakes. A favorite song, a recipe or perfume or cologne scent can help keep memories fresh.

THE FIRST ANNIVERSARY OF A loved one's death can cause memories to flood to the surface. For some, one year is a turning point, a time to celebrate life going on. Take some time to reflect. Tell God how you're feeling now. Be sure to note situations, places and things that have become easier to handle. You may want to use these pages to thank God for the healing that is taking place in your heart.

_____
_____
_____
_____
_____
_____
_____
_____
_____
_____
_____
_____
_____
_____
_____
_____
_____
_____
_____
_____
_____
_____
_____

PSALM 62:5–6

"Find Rest, O my soul, in God alone; my hope comes
from Him. He alone is my rock and my salvation;
He is my fortress, I will not be shaken."

71

THE FIRST HOLIDAYS, BIRTHDAYS AND anniversaries you experience after a death can be challenging. You may not want to celebrate the way you always have. Know that it's okay to lower your expectations, giving yourself time as you grieve the death of a loved one. Write some thoughts about this year's holidays. One of the most helpful ways to re-focus your thoughts during the holidays is to reach out to someone else. You may want to provide gifts or groceries for family in need. What are ways you might do things differently this year?

_____

_____

_____

_____

_____

_____

_____

_____

_____

_____

_____

_____

_____

_____

_____

_____

_____

_____

_____

_____

_____

_____

_____

JEREMIAH 29:11

"'For I know the plans I have for you,' declares the
Lord, 'plans to prosper you and not to harm you,
plans for hope and a future.'"

WHO HAVE BEEN YOUR "ANGELS" during this season of grief? When people pray for you, bring meals, visit, send memorials or flowers, you can feel God's touch. Remembering these acts of kindness will strengthen you today and comfort your heart in the days to come. Know that you are truly loved. On these pages, remember those who have touched your heart with genuine care and concern.

_____
_____
_____
_____
_____
_____
_____
_____
_____
_____
_____
_____
_____
_____
_____
_____
_____
_____
_____
_____
_____
_____
_____
_____
_____
_____
_____

PSALM 23:5

"...my cup overflows."

(Place a picture here

of the loved one

you are remembering

through this journal.)

MATTHEW 5:4
"Blessed are they who mourn;
for they shall be comforted."

TAKE SOME TIME TO REFLECT. Think about where you go to feel close to your loved one…maybe the beach, the mountains or the cemetery. Pray that you will sense God's presence during these times. Is there something special that you do there – leave flowers, pray, sit silently? God gave his only Son; He understands your heart. Where do you go and what do you do to reflect?

_____

_____

_____

_____

_____

_____

_____

_____

_____

_____

_____

_____

_____

_____

_____

_____

_____

_____

_____

_____

_____

_____

_____

_____

JOHN 16:22

"So with you: Now is your time of grief, but I will
see you again and you will rejoice, and no one will
take away your joy. "

MEMORIES ARE SWEET. WRITING CAN help keep things fresh in your mind. Use this page to recall some sweet, serious or hysterically funny times you had together. Laughter is good medicine!

_____
_____
_____
_____
_____
_____
_____
_____
_____
_____
_____
_____
_____
_____
_____
_____
_____
_____
_____
_____
_____
_____
_____
_____

ECCLESIASTES 3:1, 4

"There is a time for everything, and a season for every activity under heaven...a time to weep and a time to laugh; a time to mourn and a time to dance..."

ON THESE PAGES THANK GOD for His unique creation. You may want to write about the difference your loved one made in your life. Remember that every good thing—talent, personality, passion, laughter—is a gift from God. Below are a few words to help get you started.

Father, I am grateful for the life of

_____.

I thank You for Your merciful healing touch, and that You never let me go…

_____

_____

_____

_____

_____

_____

_____

_____

_____

_____

_____

_____

_____

_____

_____

_____

_____

_____

_____

_____

_____
_____
_____
_____
_____
_____
_____
_____
_____
_____
_____
_____
_____
_____
_____
_____
_____
_____
_____
_____
_____
_____
_____

PHILIPPIANS 4:8

"Finally, brothers whatever is true, whatever is noble, whatever is right, whatever is pure, whatever is lovely, whatever is admirable—if anything is excellent or praiseworthy—think about such things."

ON THESE PAGES YOU MAY want to record some favorite recipes you and your loved one shared.

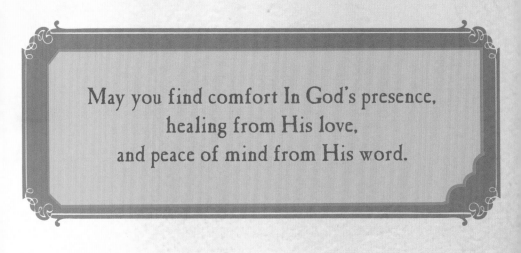

May you find comfort In God's presence,
healing from His love,
and peace of mind from His word.

IT'S HARD TO SAY EXACTLY how far this book will reach. It is my prayer that God will place it in the hands of those who need to feel His healing touch right now. The hope I share with you is of a merciful and loving God who wants to comfort you. He will sustain you and carry you through dark moments, and will be there as the light begins to shine again.

If you don't have a relationship with Jesus Christ, you can ask Him right now to come into your life. If you're ready to make this life-changing step, you may want to talk with a pastor or a friend who is a Christ-follower. I pray that if you don't have a loving church home, that the Lord would lead you to a place you can worship and grow in your faith.

May God strengthen and keep you now and always.

Beth Marshall

REVELATION 21:4

"He will wipe every tear from their eyes. There will be no more death or mourning or crying or pain, for the old order of things has passed away."

A Few Closing Thoughts

LIVING TRIBUTE

ONE COMPELLING WAY TO HONOR the memory of a special person is to create a living tribute in their name. Is there a particular cause, church, a charity or maybe a university that was significant to your loved one? If so, you might think about establishing a scholarship or an event that would raise awareness and provide funding for the cause.

Consider building a playground, donating books to a library or even planting a tree. Establishing a living tribute to your loved one can bring about healing, and will bless others for generations to come.

A Time to Heal was written as a living tribute to an unforgettable lady.

ASKING FOR HELP

There might be a day or a season when you wish you could 'check out' and somehow escape what you're feeling- pain, loneliness, anger, whatever it is. Your temptation might be to turn to alcohol, prescription medications, food, or even excessive busyness to bring some temporary relief. Although these quick fixes may provide momentary anesthesia, relying on them will inevitably leave you in worse physical and emotional shape.

Pray that God will give you His strength when you are weak. In that moment, ask Him to redirect your mind. You might want to consider taking a walk or calling a friend during a particularly difficult time. Allowing yourself to feel what you're going through, rather than masking the pain is a tough but incredibly powerful step in the healing process.

If you've slipped into a deep valley of grief and can't seem to find your way out, the most courageous move you can make is to ask for help. A pastor, Christian counselor, or local hospice organization could be a valuable resource for you.

CALL IF YOU NEED ANYTHING!

In the wake of a death, many times people want to reach out, but don't know exactly what to do. Some of the best ways to help are practical acts of kindness. A simple offer to keep children, walk a dog, cut the grass, or bring a warm meal will go a long way to relieve anxiety in the weeks following a funeral.

Many will genuinely say, "Call if you need anything." While most of us would never ask for a meal, we would be completely delighted to hear, "I have some homemade soup for you. Which night works best for me to drop it off?" A movie or restaurant gift card can be the perfect gift for a grieving person who really needs an evening out. If a practical idea comes to your mind- rather than asking what you can do, just do it!

DON'T WASTE THE PAIN

Your journey through a season of grief can equip you better than a graduate degree in counseling to be light for someone whose world seems to have gone dark. It may not be right away, but my hope is that one day you will allow God to use you and your story to inspire someone whose grief chapter has just begun.

I THANK GOD TODAY FOR my dear friend, and sister in Christ, Patti. Two years ago, Patti's beautiful twenty six year old daughter, Anne was the victim of an unthinkably violent crime that took her life. Anne was Patti's only child.

For most of us, it would seem that we might never be able to move forward after such a devastating tragedy. Is Patti's world since Anne's death forever changed? Absolutely. Patti's heart has been shattered in a way she could never have imagined. What I have seen, though in the past two years is a life that is fully dependent upon the Lord every day for His grace and strength. Patti's story is far from over.

She has made the decision to allow God to use her voice and Anne's story to share encouragement and hope with people who are hurting. Patti's life has become a powerful testimony of courage and healing. She continues to live, and wake up every morning with the assurance that God can and will bring about His goodness, even in the most heartbreaking and painful circumstances.

May this journal remind you today of God's amazing grace and love for you.

A TIME TO HEAL WAS created as a journaling guide
through the season following the death of a loved one.
The journey is bathed in healing scriptures from God's Word.
Also available from author Beth Marshall is *Seek First, A New
Believers Journal*. This journal was designed to help develop or
enhance the discipline of daily time alone with God.

To order additional copies of *A Time to Heal* please visit
www.ambassador-international.com

To order *Seek First*, please contact *and-resource@newspring.cc*